HEMP BRACELETS
and more

Easy Instructions for More Than 20 Designs

Suzanne McNeill

DESIGN ORIGINALS

an Imprint of Fox Chapel Publishing

www.d-originals.com

ACQUISITION EDITOR: Peg Couch
COPY EDITOR: Laura Taylor
COVER AND LAYOUT DESIGNER:
Ashley Millhouse
EDITOR: Katie Weeber
PHOTOGRAPHY: Lindsay Garner

Acknowledgments: Special thanks to Hemptique
(*hemptique.net*) for providing the hemp cord used
for the projects in this book.

ISBN 978-1-4972-0057-9

© 2016 by Suzanne McNeill and New Design Originals Corporation,
www.d-originals.com, an imprint of Fox Chapel Publishing, 800-457-9112,
1970 Broad Street, East Petersburg, PA 17520.

Hemp Bracelets and More is a collection of new and previously published
material. Portions of this book have been reproduced from *Hemp Happy*
(978-1-57421-116-0).

Printed in the United States of America
First printing

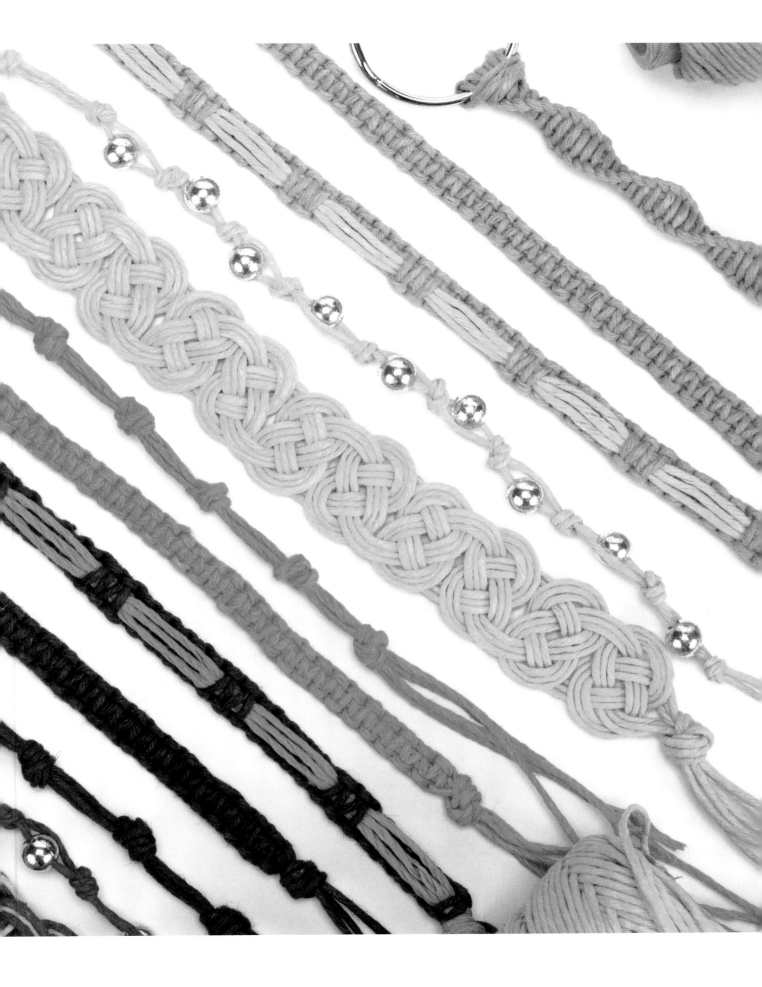

CONTENTS

Overhand Knot Bracelet **20**

Wish Bracelet **21**

Multi-Strand Overhand Knot Bracelet **22**

Overhand Knot Belt **23**

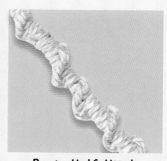

Basic Half Hitch Bracelet **26**

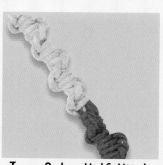

Two-Color Half Hitch Bracelet **27**

Friendship Bracelet **28**

Headphones Wrap **29**

Basic Half Knot Bracelet 32

Two-Color Half Knot Bracelet 33

Beaded Half Knot Bracelet 34

Keychain 35

Basic Square Knot Bracelet 38

Sliding Knot Bracelet 39

Striped Bracelet 40

Beaded Square Knot Bracelet 41

Basic Josephine Knot Bracelet 44

Two-Color Josephine Knot Bracelet 45

Multi-Strand Josephine Knot Bracelet 46

Josephine Knot Headband 47

There are so many cool bracelet designs you can make using hemp. Here are some ideas for inspiration. Make them your own by using your favorite colors, beads, and accessories. Have fun!

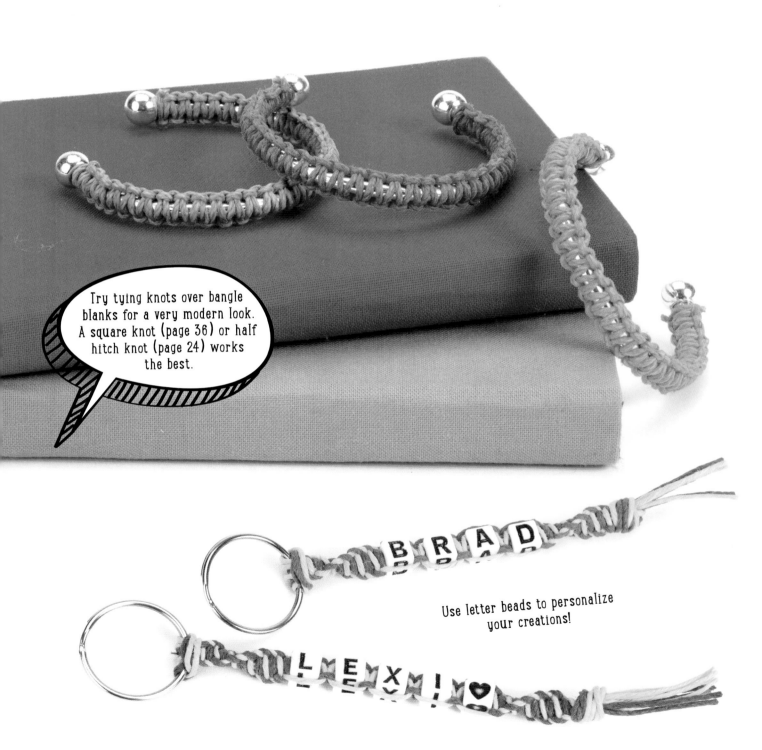

Try tying knots over bangle blanks for a very modern look. A square knot (page 36) or half hitch knot (page 24) works the best.

Use letter beads to personalize your creations!

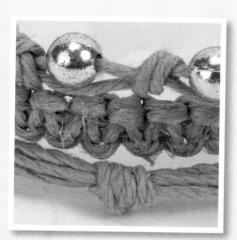

These bracelets are simple braids embellished with cute charms.

Express yourself by using letter beads to spell out something that you love, whether it's a favorite hobby, sport, or activity.

Take an ordinary braid to the next level by creating an alternating color pattern.

Create an elegant multistrand bracelet using a dual-ended connector and simple beads.

Make a set of bracelets by using hemp in one color and switching up your embellishments.

8   HEMP BRACELETS AND MORE

Make multiples of the same bracelet design in complementary colors so you can stack them high on your wrists!

GETTING STARTED

Working with hemp is super easy! You only need a few supplies to start making some really cool designs. Read through this section to learn the basics. Then turn to page 16 to start putting your knowledge to use by making some projects.

Tools and Materials

Hemp cord. Did you know that hemp is a plant? And it can be used to make all kinds of useful things like cloth, paper, wax, and, of course, rope! Hemp was once used to make all of the ropes on sailing ships. The hemp cord you'll use for jewelry making is much thinner than a ship's ropes, but it's just as strong. You'll find the projects you make using hemp cord can withstand a lot of wear and tear and will last a long time.

Hemp cord can be found in the jewelry section of your local craft store. It's often available in different thicknesses and a rainbow of colors. You might find the cord feels different depending on the process used to make it and whether or not it has been dyed. Some hemp cord will feel stiff, while other cord will feel soft and flexible, like string. You can use any type of hemp cord for the projects in this book.

Scissors. You'll want a nice pair of scissors to cut and trim your hemp cord. Dull scissors might leave you with frayed cord ends.

Ruler or yardstick. You'll often need several feet of hemp for each project, so you'll want a ruler on hand. A yardstick can be very useful for measuring long strands of hemp.

Glue. You can use glue to give knots extra security or to secure loose ends in a design.

Clipboard. This is not a necessity, but a clipboard can be helpful. Use the clip to hold down one end of your design while you knot your way to the other end.

Beads, rings, and charms. Hemp looks great on its own, but you can also embellish your designs with beads and charms. Tie hemp onto a key ring to make a keychain—there are lots of possibilities. When purchasing beads and charms, check the size of the holes—you'll want to make sure they're large enough to thread onto your hemp cord without getting stuck.

Simple Knots

Here are some simple knots that you can incorporate into your designs. A lark's head knot allows you to attach your design to other items, like a key ring, zipper, or charm. A basic braid is a nice way to start or end a design, or it can make a nice design all on its own.

LARK'S HEAD KNOT

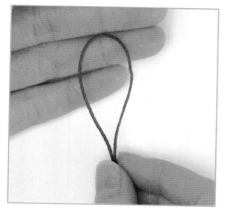

Fold the strand in half. This will form a loop at the center. Hold on to the center loop.

Place the center loop under the item you're attaching the hemp to (like a key ring).

Bring the ends of the hemp around the item and down through the center loop. Pull tight, and the hemp will be snugly attached to your item.

BASIC BRAID

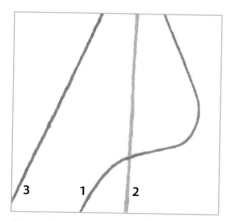

Start with three strands. Bring the right strand (1) over the center strand (2).

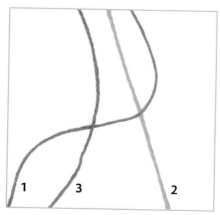

Then bring the left strand (3) over the new center strand (1).

Starting and Finishing a Bracelet

The designs in this book primarily use overhand knots with loops or long tails to start and finish a bracelet, but you can use any of the methods described here depending on the look you're going for.

Overhand knot. An overhand knot (see page 18) can be used to tie multiple strands together at the beginning or end of a bracelet. If you use a regular overhand knot without a loop, you'll probably want to leave long tails or make a braid so you will have something to tie the bracelet onto your wrist with.

Overhand knot with loop. By folding the strands for your bracelet in half, you will make a loop at the center. Tie an overhand knot with this loop (see page 18) and you will have a bracelet that has a loop at one end to act as a closure.

Long tails. You can leave long tails at one or both ends of your bracelet to tie the bracelet onto your wrist. To keep your knotwork from unraveling, tie the strands together in an overhand knot before you trim the tails. You can also tie an overhand knot at the end of each tail to prevent fraying.

Basic braid. You can make a braid at one or both ends of your bracelet to tie the bracelet onto your wrist. To hold the braids in place, you'll need to tie an overhand knot at the beginning and end.

Button or bead closure. If your bracelet has a loop at one end, you can add a bead or button at the other end to act as a closure. Tie the bead or button onto the end of the bracelet and slide it through the loop at the other end to close.

Jewelry Findings

You don't need to use jewelry findings for the projects in this book. It's easy to create closures using the hemp itself and to add beads or charms by threading them onto the strands in your design. Jewelry findings can give your project a more polished look and some added durability. If you decide you'd like to add some jewelry components to your designs, here are some helpful tips.

FOLD-OVER CRIMPS

Fold-over crimps finish the ends of a project by holding all of the strands together. The crimps also have loops on the ends for attaching clasps.

JUMP RINGS

Jump rings allow you to connect different jewelry elements, like a clasp and a fold-over crimp or a charm and another charm.

Place the strands at one end of your bracelet into the fold-over crimp. Use jewelry pliers to fold down one side of the crimp.

Use two pairs of jewelry pliers to open a jump ring. Position the jump ring with the opening at the top, and use each pair of pliers to grip the ring on either side of the opening.

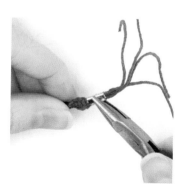

Fold down the second side of the crimp to secure the ends in place. Trim away the tails.

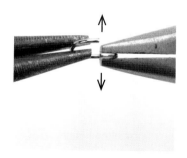

Open the jump ring by gently twisting your wrists. Twist one hand toward yourself, and the other hand away. To close the jump ring, slowly twist it back the opposite direction you opened it.

Repeat with a second ribbon crimp on the other end of the bracelet. Use jump rings (see at right) to attach one half of a clasp to each end of the bracelet.

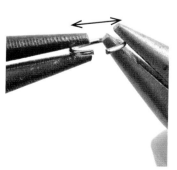

Don't try to open the jump ring by pulling the two halves away from each other left and right. Doing this makes the ring lose its shape and can weaken the metal. Similarly, do not try to squeeze a jump ring closed using one pair of pliers.

All About Color

At one time, it was rare to find hemp cord in more than a few basic colors. Now you can find hemp in any color you can imagine and in some unique variations, like metallic and variegated cord. All of these choices are awesome, but they can make it hard to pick the colors you want to use for a project! Don't worry, it's easy to pick colors when you think about what they mean to you. What are the colors of your favorite sports team or superhero? What about the colors of your school? If you wanted to make a princess bracelet, what colors would you pick? What colors would you use for a bracelet based on a video game character? Below is a list of colors and some of the words associated with them. Try making a bracelet that sends a message with the colors you choose.

Red
- Daring
- Love
- Excitement
- Energy

Orange
- Health
- Happiness
- Courage
- Creativity

Yellow
- Joy
- Friendliness
- Warmth
- Optimism

Blue
- Peace
- Serenity
- Confidence
- Trust

Green
- Growth
- Balance
- Soothing
- Nature

Purple
- Creativity
- Dignity
- Wisdom
- Ambition

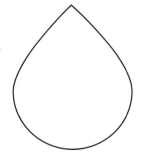

White
- Hope
- Purity
- Simplicity
- Light

Black
- Bold
- Mystery
- Elegance
- Strength

If you're still not sure what colors you'd like to use, check out these color combos based on different themes. Which ones are your favorites?

Sports Teams
- Red/Blue
- Black/Yellow
- Blue/White
- Purple/Yellow

Superheroes
- Red/Blue
- Green/Purple
- Red/Yellow
- Black/Green

Holidays and Seasons
- Red/Green
- Black/Orange
- Yellow/Green
- White/Blue

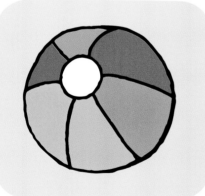

Color Wheel
- Blue/Orange
- Yellow/Purple
- Pink/Green
- Black/White

I'm a Princess
- White/Purple
- Pink/Purple
- Pink/White
- Purple/Yellow

Boys Rule
- Blue/Orange
- Black/Red
- Light Blue/Dark Blue
- Red/Orange

THE PROJECTS

There are so many cool projects that you can make with hemp. And the best part is you can customize each one to match your own style and personality through the colors you select and the embellishments you use. If your style is fun and funky, try neon colors and bright, shiny beads. If you like a boho look, try neutrals or natural–colored hemp with wooden beads. If you want something simple and chic, try hemp in metallic varieties with subtle metallic beads. There are endless opportunities to show off your taste and style. Have fun making these projects your own!

OVERHAND KNOT

HOW TO DO IT:

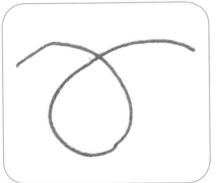

1 Cross the ends of the strand to form a loop.

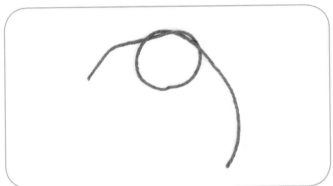

2 Take the top working strand and feed it through the loop, from bottom to top. Pull tight.

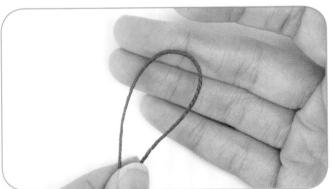

3 To form an overhand knot with a loop at the top, fold the working strands in half first to form a loop at the center.

4 Repeat the steps above to form an overhand knot.

Overhand Knot Bracelet

MATERIALS
• **Two 2' (60cm) strands of hemp**

1 Fold the strands in half to form a loop at the center.

2 Tie the strands in an overhand knot with a loop at the top (see page 18).

3 Tie a second overhand knot about ½" (1.5cm) from the first. Repeat until the bracelet reaches the desired length.

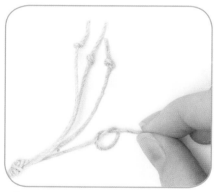

4 Trim the tails of the bracelet to about 2" (5cm) in length. Tie an overhand knot at the end of each tail to prevent fraying.

Switch it up!
Try this bracelet with more strands, or use strands in different colors. This design also looks great with metallic hemp.

Wish Bracelet

MATERIALS

- One 2' (60cm) strand of hemp
- About ten ³⁄₁₆" (5mm) beads

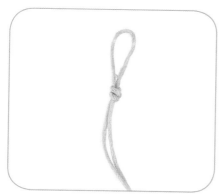

1 Fold the strand in half to form a loop at the center. Tie the strand in an overhand knot with a loop at the top (see page 18).

2 Tie a second overhand knot about ½" (1.5cm) from the first. Slide a bead onto one of the strands.

3 Continue tying overhand knots every ½" (1.5cm) and adding a bead to one strand between each knot until the bracelet reaches the desired length. Finish with an overhand knot.

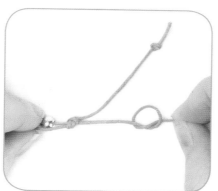

4 Trim the tails of the bracelet to about 2" (5cm) in length. Tie an overhand knot at the end of each tail to prevent fraying.

Switch it up!
Use a variety of beads to create different styles. Try shiny beads for a glam look, wooden beads for a boho look, or bright neons for a fresh, modern look.

Make a Wish!
Make a wish when you tie on this bracelet. When the hemp wears out and you lose the beads, your wish is sent out to the world and is believed to come true!

Multi-Strand Overhand Knot Bracelet

MATERIALS

- Four 2' (60cm) strands of hemp
- About 30 beads of your choice

1 Using an overhand knot, tie all four strands together at one end, 4" (10cm) from the end.

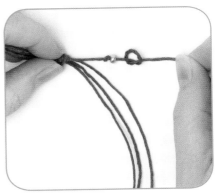

2 Tie an overhand knot in one strand about ½" (1.5cm) away from the knot you used to tie all the strands together. Thread a bead onto the strand. Tie an overhand knot immediately after the bead.

3 Repeat, using random spacing, until you have a beaded section about 6" (15cm) long. Repeat with the remaining three strands.

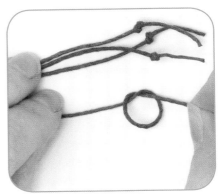

4 Tie the four strands together after the beaded sections using an overhand knot. Trim the ends to about 4" (10cm) long. Tie an overhand knot at the end of each tail at both ends of the bracelet to prevent fraying.

Overhand Knot Belt

MATERIALS

- **Four 8' (250cm) strands of hemp**

1 Using an overhand knot, tie all four strands together at one end, 8" (20.5cm) from the end.

2 Take the two left strands and tie them together using an overhand knot, about 1" (2.5cm) from the first knot. Repeat with the two right strands.

3 Take the two center strands and tie them together using an overhand knot, about 1" (2.5cm) from the last set of knots.

4 Repeat Steps 2–3 until the belt reaches the desired length. To finish, tie all four strands together using an overhand knot and trim the tails to about 8" (20.5cm). Tie an overhand knot at the end of each tail to prevent fraying.

Switch it up!
Try adding beads to this design. They look especially great added to the tails at each end of the belt.

HALF HITCH KNOT

HOW TO DO IT:

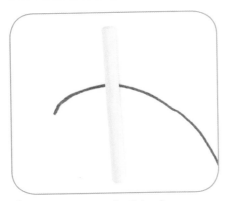

1 Place one end of the hemp under the item you are wrapping (like headphones or another strand of hemp). This is the starting end. The remaining long end is the working end.

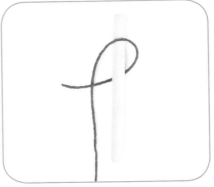

2 Bring the long working end of the cord around the short starting end. This will form a loop around the item you are wrapping.

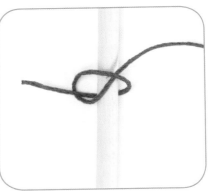

3 Bring the working end through the loop you made in Step 2.

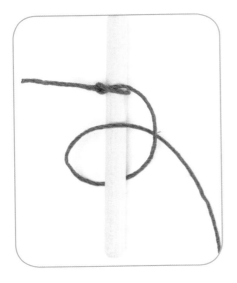

4 You'll make your next knot under the first one. Bring the working end around the item you are wrapping to start forming a loop. Feed the working end of the cord through the loop to finish it. Tighten the loop.

5 Repeat Step 4, bringing the working end around the item you are wrapping and feeding it through the loop that forms.

Basic Half Hitch Bracelet

MATERIALS
• Two 8' (250cm) strands of hemp

1 Fold the strands in half to form a loop at the center. Tie the strands in an overhand knot with a loop at the top (see page 18).

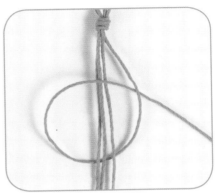

2 Tie a half hitch knot. Take any strand, bring it around all the other strands to form a loop, and feed the end through the loop.

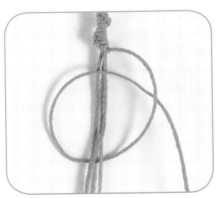

3 You'll make the next knot under the first one. Continue making half hitch knots until the bracelet reaches the desired length.

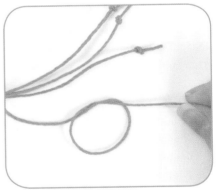

4 Tie all the strands together in an overhand knot. Trim the tails to about 2" (5cm) in length. Tie an overhand knot at the end of each tail to prevent fraying.

Switch it up!
You can add beads to this design in a few different ways. Try threading a bead onto the working strand each time you make a half hitch, or thread a bead onto all four strands at once.

Two-Color Half Hitch Bracelet

MATERIALS

- One 6' (180cm) strand of hemp in Color 1
- One 6' (180cm) strand of hemp in Color 2

Switch it up! Add more strands to this design for more colors! Or try using variegated hemp.

1 Fold the strands in half to form a loop at the center. Tie the strands in an overhand knot with a loop at the top (see page 18).

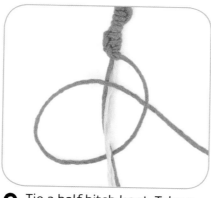

2 Tie a half hitch knot. Take a strand in Color 1, bring it around all the other strands to form a loop, and feed the end through the loop. Continue tying half hitches with Color 1 for about 1" (2.5cm).

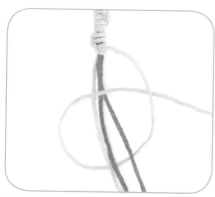

3 Take a strand in Color 2, bring it around all the other strands to form a loop, and feed the end through the loop. Continue tying half hitches with Color 2 for about 1" (2.5cm).

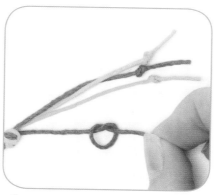

4 Continue tying half hitches, alternating colors, until the bracelet reaches the desired length. Tie all the strands together in an overhand knot. Trim the tails to about 2" (5cm) in length. Tie an overhand knot at the end of each tail to prevent fraying.

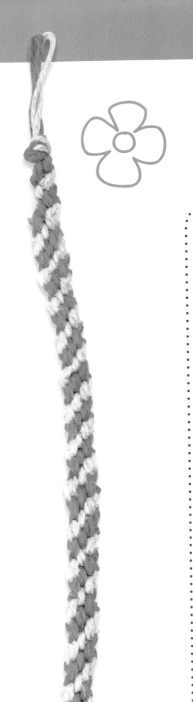

Friendship Bracelet

MATERIALS

- One 10' (300cm) strand of hemp in Color 1
- One 10' (300cm) strand of hemp in Color 2

1 Fold the strands in half to form a loop at the center. Tie the strands in an overhand knot with a loop at the top (see page 18). Arrange the strands so that the colors alternate.

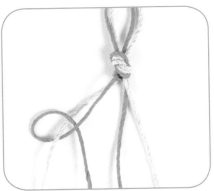

2 Take the first strand on the left and use it to tie two half hitches onto the strand next to it. This will move the strand from left to right.

3 Use the same strand to tie two half hitches onto the next strand to the right, and then onto the last strand on the right. The strand that started out as the first strand on the left should now be the last strand on the right.

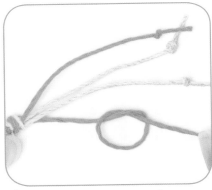

4 Repeat Steps 2–3, using the far left strand to tie half hitches across all the other strands. Repeat until the bracelet reaches the desired length. Tie all the strands together in an overhand knot. Trim the tails to about 2" (5cm) in length. Tie an overhand knot at the end of each tail to prevent fraying.

Switch it up!

In Step 1, arrange the strands so the Color 1 strands are on the left and the Color 2 strands are on the right to create thick stripes.

Headphones Wrap

MATERIALS
- One 40' (1.25m) strand of hemp in Color 1
- One 20' (0.75m) strand of hemp in Color 2
- One 20' (0.75m) strand of hemp in Color 3

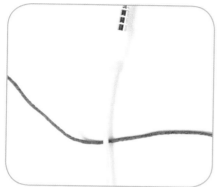

1 This wrap is made using a half hitch as shown on page 24. To start, place one end of the Color 1 strand under your headphone cord near the plug. The end under your headphone cord is the starting end. The remaining long end is the working end.

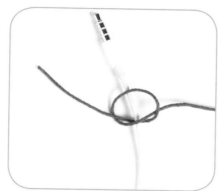

2 Bring the long working end around the short starting end. This will form a loop around the headphone cord. Bring the working end through this loop.

Switch it up!
You can use as many colors as you want. Follow Steps 1–3 to start a color. When you want to switch colors, simply start a new cord following the same steps.

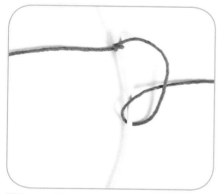

3 You'll make your next knot under the first one. Bring the working end around the headphone cord to form a loop and feed the end through the loop. Continue tying half hitches with Color 1 until you reach the point where the headphone cord splits.

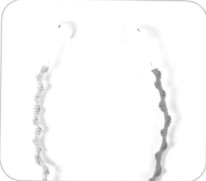

4 Following Steps 1–3, use the Color 2 strand to wrap the left cord from the point where the cord splits all the way to the earbud. Use the Color 3 strand to wrap the right cord. If your headphones have a volume control button, stop the wrap before it (see Step 5) and continue after it (see Steps 1–3).

5 Trim all of the tails and cover them with glue to hold them in place.

HALF KNOT

HOW TO DO IT:

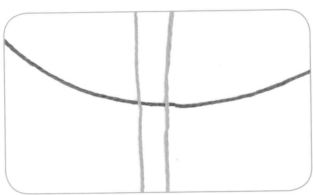

1 In this book, you will always make a half knot over filler strands. Take two strands (the filler strands) and place them side by side. Take the strand you will tie the knots with (the working strand) and place it under the filler strands, making a plus sign as shown.

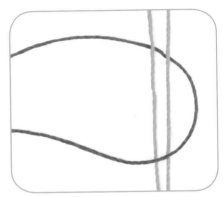

2 Bring the right working strand over the filler strands.

3 Bring the left working strand over the right working strand, under the filler strands, and over and through the loop formed by the right working strand.

4 Repeat Steps 2–3, always bringing the right strand over the filler strands. Tying this knot will naturally cause the working strands to twist around the filler strands, forming a spiral shape.

www.Hemptique.net
Premium Quality Crafting Cord

Switch it up!
Try adding beads to this design by sliding them onto both filler strands at once before you tie a knot.

Basic Half Knot Bracelet

MATERIALS

• Two 8' (250cm) strands of hemp

1 Fold the strands in half to form a loop at the center. Tie the strands in an overhand knot with a loop at the top (see page 18).

2 Start tying a half knot. Bring the right working strand over the filler strands. Then bring the left working strand over the right working strand, under the filler strands, and over and through the loop formed by the right working strand. Tighten the knot.

3 Repeat Step 2 to continue tying half knots until the bracelet reaches the desired length.

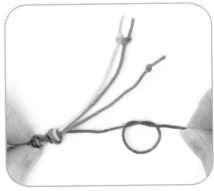

4 Tie all the strands together in an overhand knot. Trim the tails to about 2" (5cm) in length. Tie an overhand knot at the end of each tail to prevent fraying.

Two-Color Half Knot Bracelet

MATERIALS

- One 8' (250cm) strand of hemp in Color 1
- One 8' (250cm) strand of hemp in Color 2

1 Fold the strands in half to form a loop at the center. Tie the strands in an overhand knot with a loop at the top (see page 18).

2 Tie a half knot with the Color 1 strands. Bring the right Color 1 strand over the Color 2 strands. Then bring the left Color 1 strand over the right Color 1 strand, under the Color 2 strands, and over and through the loop formed by the right Color 1 strand. Tighten the knot.

3 Repeat Step 2 to continue tying half knots with Color 1 for about 1" (2.5cm). Then, switch colors by using the strands in Color 2 to tie half knots over the strands in Color 1. Continue for about 1" (2.5cm).

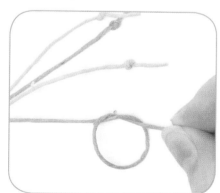

4 Repeat Steps 2–3 until the bracelet reaches the desired length. Tie all the strands together in an overhand knot. Trim the tails to about 2" (5cm) in length. Tie an overhand knot at the end of each tail to prevent fraying.

Switch it up!
You can switch colors randomly if you'd like to create a more abstract pattern.

Beaded Half Knot Bracelet

MATERIALS

- **Two 8' (250cm) strands of hemp**
- **Five ⅜" (10mm) beads**

1 Fold the strands in half to form a loop at the center. Tie the strands in an overhand knot with a loop at the top (see page 18).

2 Start tying a half knot. Bring the right working strand over the filler strands. Then bring the left working strand over the right working strand, under the filler strands, and over and through the loop formed by the right working strand. Tighten the knot. Repeat, tying fourteen more half knots.

3 Thread a bead onto both filler strands, then tie fifteen half knots. Repeat, adding a bead every fifteen knots until all five beads have been added. After the last bead, tie fifteen half knots.

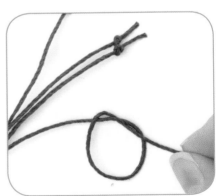

4 Tie all the strands together in an overhand knot. Trim the tails to about 2" (5cm) in length. Tie an overhand knot at the end of each tail to prevent fraying.

Switch it up!
To make this bracelet shorter or longer, adjust the number of half knots you tie at the beginning and end and/or between each bead.

Keychain

MATERIALS
- **Four 6' (180cm) strands of hemp**
- **Three ½" (15mm) beads**
- **1 key ring**

1 Fold the strands in half to form a loop at the center. Tie the strands onto the key ring using a lark's head knot (see page 11).

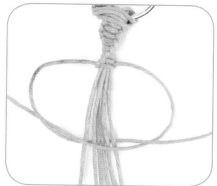

2 Start tying a half knot. Bring the right working strand over the filler strands. Then bring the left working strand over the right working strand, under the filler strands, and over and through the loop formed by the right working strand. Tighten the knot. Repeat, tying nine more half knots.

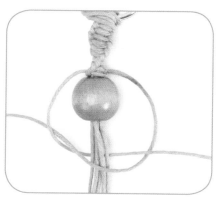

3 Thread a bead onto all of the filler strands at once, then tie ten half knots. Repeat until all three beads have been added. Tie one half knot after the last bead.

4 Tie all the strands together in an overhand knot. Trim the tails to about 2" (5cm) in length. Tie an overhand knot at the end of each tail to prevent fraying.

Switch it up!
Use this keychain to highlight some of your favorite things. Pick themed beads with designs that show off your personality and interests. Look for sports balls, music notes, flowers, letters, and more.

SQUARE KNOT

HOW TO DO IT:

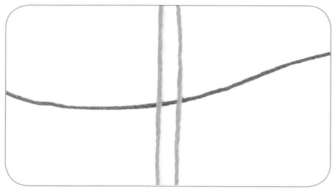

1 In this book, you will always make a square knot over filler strands. To start, take two filler strands and place them side by side. Take the strand you will tie the knots with (this is called the working strand) and place it under the filler strands, making a plus sign as shown.

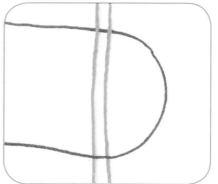

2 Bring the right working strand over the filler strands.

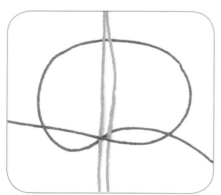

3 Bring the left working strand over the right working strand, under the filler strands, and over and through the loop formed by the right working strand. Tighten.

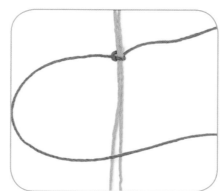

4 Bring the new left working strand over the filler strands.

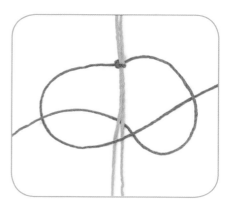

5 Bring the right working strand over the left working strand, under the filler strand, and over and through the loop formed by the left working strand.

Basic Square Knot Bracelet

MATERIALS

- One 8' (250cm) strand of hemp in Color 1
- One 8' (250cm) strand of hemp in Color 2

1 Fold the strands in half to form a loop at the center. Tie the strands in an overhand knot with a loop at the top (see page 18). Arrange the strands so the colors alternate.

2 Start tying a square knot. Bring the right working strand over the filler strands. Then bring the left working strand over the right working strand, under the filler strands, and over and through the loop formed by the right working strand. Tighten the knot.

3 Finish tying the square knot. Bring the left working strand over the filler strands. Then, bring the right working strand over the left working strand, under the filler strands, and over and through the loop formed by the left working strand. Tighten the knot.

4 Repeat Steps 2–3 to continue tying square knots until the bracelet reaches the desired length. Tie all the strands together in an overhand knot. Trim the tails to about 2" (5cm) in length. Tie an overhand knot at the end of each tail to prevent fraying.

Switch it up!

In this design, the working strand that crosses over the filler strands (the right working strand) will appear at the center of the finished bracelet; the strand that crosses under the filler strands (the left working strand) will appear at the outside of the finished bracelet. To change where the colors appear, change the order of the strands in Step 1.

Sliding Knot Bracelet

MATERIALS

- Two 12" (30.5cm) strands of hemp
- One 6" (15cm) strand of hemp
- 1 dual-ended connector charm
- Glue

Switch it up!
Try purchasing a set of charms with a common theme, such as a nautical theme, and use them to make multiple bracelets.

1 Fold one of the 12" (30.5cm) strands in half to form a loop at the center. Attach the strand to one end of the charm using a lark's head knot (see page 11). Repeat with the remaining 12" (30.5cm) strand on the other end of the charm.

2 Arrange the strands attached to the charm in a circle. Place the 6" (15cm) strand under the bracelet's strands directly opposite the charm where they cross. Tie a square knot with the 6" (15cm) strand over the bracelet strands (see page 36).

3 Finish tying the square knot. Bring the left working strand over the filler strands. Then bring the right working strand over the left working strand, under the filler strands, and over and through the loop formed by the left working strand. Repeat Steps 2–3 to tie two more square knots with the 6" (15cm) strand.

4 Trim the tails of the 6" (15cm) strand and cover them with glue. Tie each pair of bracelet strands together in an overhand knot and trim the ends.

Striped Bracelet

MATERIALS

- One 8' (250cm) strand of hemp in Color 1
- Three 8' (250cm) strands of hemp in Color 2

1 Fold all of the strands in half to form a loop at the center. Tie the strands in an overhand knot with a loop at the top (see page 18).

2 Use the strands in Color 1 to tie two square knots over the strands in Color 2 (see page 36).

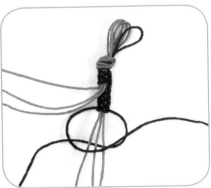

3 Move three of the Color 2 strands to the side. Use the Color 1 strands to tie five square knots over the remaining three Color 2 strands.

4 Bring all of the Color 2 strands back together. Use the Color 1 strands to tie two square knots over all of the Color 2 strands.

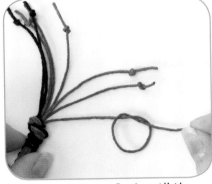

5 Repeat Steps 3–4 until the bracelet reaches the desired length. Tie all the strands together in an overhand knot. Trim the tails to about 2" (5cm) in length. Tie an overhand knot at the end of each tail to prevent fraying.

Switch it up!
Use up to four different colors in this design to create multicolor stripes.

Beaded Square Knot Bracelet

MATERIALS

- **Two 8' (250cm) strands of hemp**
- **About five ⅜" (10mm) beads**
- **About thirty-six 6/0 seed beads**

1 Fold the strands in half to form a loop at the center. Tie the strands in an overhand knot with a loop at the top (see page 18).

2 Take the two outer strands and use them as working strands to tie a square knot over the filler strands. Thread a seed bead onto each working strand. Tie a square knot. Repeat twice more so that four square knots have been tied with a set of beads between each knot.

3 Thread both filler strands through a ⅜" (1cm) bead.

Switch it up!

Make a two-color bracelet by using hemp in two different colors for the working strands.

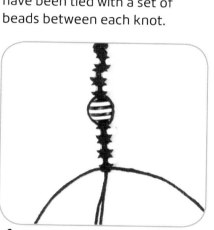

4 Take the two outer strands and use them as working strands to tie a square knot over the filler strands. Thread a seed bead onto each working strand. Tie a square knot. Repeat twice more so that four square knots have been tied with a set of beads between each knot.

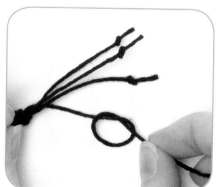

5 Repeat Steps 3–4 until the bracelet reaches the desired length. Tie all the strands together in an overhand knot. Trim the tails to about 2" (5cm) in length. Tie an overhand knot at the end of each tail to prevent fraying.

JOSEPHINE KNOT

HOW TO DO IT:

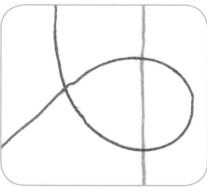

1 Start with two strands side by side. Use the left working strand to form a loop on top of the right working strand.

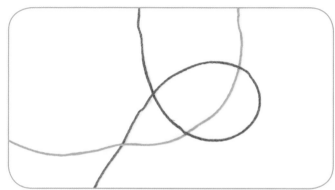

2 Bring the end of the right working strand over the end of the left working strand.

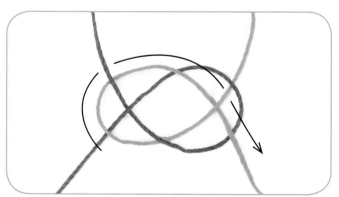

3 Feed the right working strand through the knot as shown, following an alternating under-over pattern.

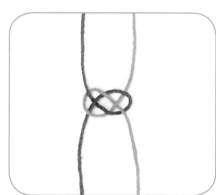

4 Pull on the starting and working ends of the strands to close and shape the knot.

Basic Josephine Knot Bracelet
MATERIALS
- **One 6' (180cm) strand of hemp**

1 Fold the strand in half to form a loop at the center. Tie the strand in an overhand knot with a loop at the top (see page 18).

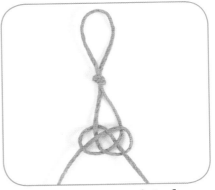

2 Use the two strands to form a Josephine knot. Use the left working strand to form a loop on top of the right working strand. Bring the end of the right working strand over the end of the left working strand. Feed the right working strand through the knot as shown on page 42. Pull on the strands gently to close and shape the knot.

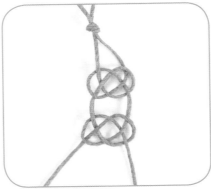

3 Leave about ½" (1.5cm) of space and tie another Josephine knot. Repeat until the bracelet reaches the desired length.

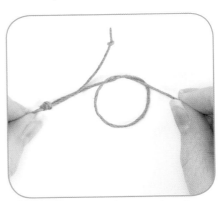

4 Tie the strands together in an overhand knot. Trim the tails to about 2" (5cm) in length. Tie an overhand knot at the end of each tail to prevent fraying.

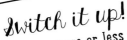

Switch it up!
You can leave more or less space between the knots, and you can leave the knots loose or tighten them so they are small and dense.

Two-Color Josephine Knot Bracelet

MATERIALS
- One 3' (90cm) strand of hemp in Color 1
- One 3' (90cm) strand of hemp in Color 2

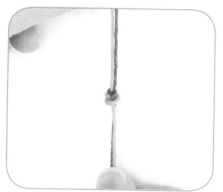

1 Using an overhand knot, tie the two strands together at one end, 4" (10cm) from the end.

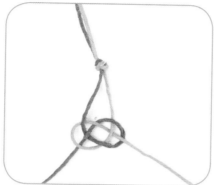

2 Use the two strands to form a Josephine knot. Use the left working strand to form a loop on top of the right working strand. Bring the end of the right working strand over the end of the left working strand. Feed the right working strand through the knot as shown. Pull on the strands gently to close and shape the knot.

3 Leave about ½" (1.5cm) of space and tie another Josephine knot. Repeat until the bracelet reaches the desired length.

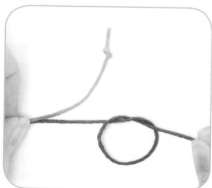

4 Tie the strands together after the knotted section using an overhand knot. Trim the ends to about 4" (10cm) long. You will have two tails at each end of the bracelet. Tie an overhand knot at the end of each one to prevent fraying.

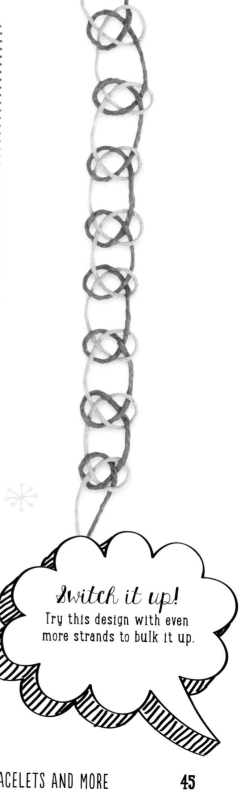

Switch it up!
Try this design with even more strands to bulk it up.

Multi-Strand Josephine Knot Bracelet

MATERIALS

• **Three 12' (370cm) strands of hemp**

1 Fold the strands in half to form a loop at the center. Tie the strands in an overhand knot with a loop at the top (see page 18).

2 Separate the strands into two groups of three. Use the two groups to form a Josephine knot. Use the left working strands to form a loop on top of the right working strands. Bring the ends of the right working strands over the ends of the left working strands. Feed the right working strands through the knot as shown. Pull on the strands gently to close and shape the knot.

3 Leave a little space and tie another Josephine knot. Repeat until the bracelet reaches the desired length.

4 Tie the strands together in an overhand knot. Trim the tails to about 2" (5cm) in length. Tie an overhand knot at the end of each tail to prevent fraying.

Josephine Knot Headband

MATERIALS

- **Twelve 1½' (45cm) strands of hemp**
- **Headband**
- **Glue**

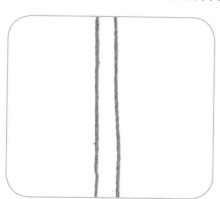

1 Take two strands and place them side–by–side.

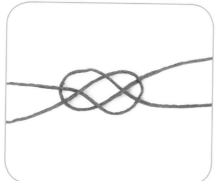

2 Use the two strands to form a Josephine knot (see page 42). Use the left working strand to form a loop on top of the right working strand. Bring the end of the right working strand over the end of the left working strand. Feed the right working strand through the knot as shown. Keep the knot loose for now.

3 Take two more strands and feed them through the knot you made in Step 2, following the pattern. Repeat until you have added all of the strands to the knot. Gently pull on the strands to close and shape the knot.

4 Trim the ends of the strands and glue them in place. Glue the knot to a purchased headband. Depending on the thickness of the headband, you might be able to slide the knot onto it.

Switch it up!
You can use strands in different colors to create a cool color pattern for this design.

KNOT DIRECTORY

Lark's Head Knot. page 11

Basic Braid. page 11

Overhand Knot. page 18

Half Hitch Knot. page 24

Half Knot. page 30

Square Knot. page 36

Josephine Knot. page 42